Poetry That Touches the Heart

"Her poems are witty and pithy, like a haiku that lingers in the mind long after it has been read."
— *San Francisco Examiner*

"I've seen Natasha's audiences burst into laughter, cheers, and applause at her verse. She captures the hopes and aspirations that are so much a part of modern women's lives, and she captures it all with marvelous humor."
— *Washington Post*

"One of America's most gifted poets."
— Warren Farrell,
author of *The Liberated Male* and
Why Men Are The Way They Are

"She writes from a perspective of having been there and completing the task — wife, mother, grandmother, professional. When she speaks or writes, she's answering women's concerns.... Her poems offer observations and comfort."
— *Salt Lake Tribune*

"Natasha Josefowitz's verse says it all for the men and women of today.... It is delightful and provides new awarenesses with each reading. Natasha's personhood is embodied in each thought. It is brilliant!"
— Dr. Janet D. Greenwood,
President, Longwood College, Virginia

Also by Natasha Josefowitz

IS THIS WHERE I WAS GOING? *
          (light verse)
PATHS TO POWER: A Woman's Guide
          from First Job to Top
          Executive
YOU'RE THE BOSS! A Guide to
          Managing People with
          Understanding and
          Effectiveness *

*published by Warner Books.

NATASHA'S WORDS FOR FRIENDS

NATASHA JOSEFOWITZ

DRAWINGS BY
MARY MIETZELFELD

WARNER BOOKS

A Warner Communications Company

This book is part of a trilogy. The other two
by the same author are:

Natasha's Words for Lovers
Natasha's Words for Families

Copyright © 1986 by Natasha Josefowitz
All rights reserved.
Warner Books, Inc., 666 Fifth Avenue, New York, NY 10103

W A Warner Communications Company

Printed in the United States of America
First Printing: November 1986
10 9 8 7 6 5 4 3 2

Cover design by Mary Mietzelfeld

Library of Congress Cataloging-in-Publication Data

Josefowitz, Natasha.
  Natasha's words for friends.

  1. Friendship — Poetry. I. Title.
PS3560.0768N35 1986   811'.54   86-9244
ISBN 0-446-38295-7 (U.S.A.) (pbk.)
      0-446-38296-5 (Canada) (pbk.)

To my women friends whose experiences are also part of this book:

Miriam Polster for all the laughing we do together,

Marjorie Shaevitz for the sharing of both our personal and our professional lives,

Alice Sargent for her support and generosity through the years,

Maxine Kleinberg for the steadfastness of forty-six years of friendship,

Jean Wells, former roommate and still close friend despite time and distance,

and to all those whose phone calls, visits and love have warmed me throughout the years.

A special thanks to my editor, Fredda
Isaacson, vice-president of Warner Books,
who began as my greatest supporter five
books ago and who has become a very dear
friend.

Much appreciation to Lily Turner for
typing, filing and refiling hundreds of
poems — always with a smile; and to
Monica Elias and Barbara White for
their contributions to the illustrations.

While some of the verses are
autobiographical, many reflect the feelings
and experiences of friends and colleagues. I
am grateful for their sharing them with me
and making this book richer.

Contents

Introduction

This book is written for friends everywhere, with whom we share so much of our lives, with whom we go shopping, sit on park benches, have lunch, go to movies, talk on the phone for hours, share confidences, argue, get angry, and whom we forgive and who forgive us.

This book is also written for the colleagues we work with, the bosses we work for, and the staff who report to us.

Many of us spend most of our days at work, and in these pages we celebrate those people who make our jobs a little easier by helping us survive or just by keeping us sane.

The Visit

Good friends
coming to stay
for a week
I'm pleased
and I'm not
If I could only say
"There's the fridge
Help yourselves
I'll fix my own later"
it would be easy
but instead
I market, cook
set tables, serve
clean up
saying, "No, no, don't help,
I'd really rather do it myself"
When they do help
I can't find anything afterwards
yet if they don't
I bang around the kitchen
resenting them.

Best Friends

I have some friends I never see
who live thousands of miles away
we were best friends in college
or when our children were small

but now we call each other only
when we have good news
or when we're unhappy
or just need to reconnect

Neither the distance nor the years
seem to matter
we can start right up
where we left off
When there is no other way
good friends should be heard
if they can't be seen.

Bargains!

I love to buy
but I hate to spend

so I go to discount stores
warehouse clearances
bargain basements
special sales
closeouts

and come home with things
that end up
in garage sales
charity bazaars
the Salvation Army
and other places
where people go
who love to buy
but hate to spend.

Wrong Sizes

If short women are discounted
and tall women are threatening
average women are invisible
all that's left is men,
whose looks or sizes
never seem to matter.

First Times

I wish I never had to do
anything for the first time
it makes me too anxious

I wish I could always start
by doing everything
the second time.

Reality

When I am nice and sweet
compliant and kind
when I give in
I am discounted
I get taken advantage of
when I'm a doormat
I get walked on

When I am difficult
demanding and angry
when I won't compromise
I am respected and deferred to
I am taken into account
and when I'm most tough
I'm listened to

Must I change what I am
becoming what I don't
want to be
to get what I need?

Tomorrow I Will Change

Tomorrow I will change
turn a new leaf
become this new person

I will exercise before breakfast
not eat cookies between meals
not fret over trivialities
not run about
getting upset
that I'm not getting
everything done

Tomorrow I will change.

I say this every day.

No Words Needed

She's selling pretzels
at a corner stand
I smile
and she smiles back
We know

She ambles past me
lugging three big shopping bags
our eyes meet
we sigh
We know

At the bus stop
she's holding on to screaming children
we look at each other
and wink
We know

She rushes by
carrying a briefcase
we exchange glances
of recognition
We know

Some man is making
a pass at her
she shrugs her shoulders
we laugh
We know

A woman with hair
as grey as mine
stares at me
we nod
We know

We pass one another
on the street
women who don't know
each other
Yet we know.

Bodies

Some bodies are made
for bathing suits
> **others look best
> in formals**

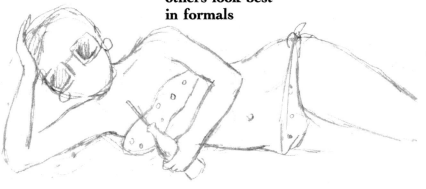

Some bodies are made
for very tight pants
> **others must wear
> skirts**

Some bodies are made
for tailored suits
> **others for
> frilly blouses**

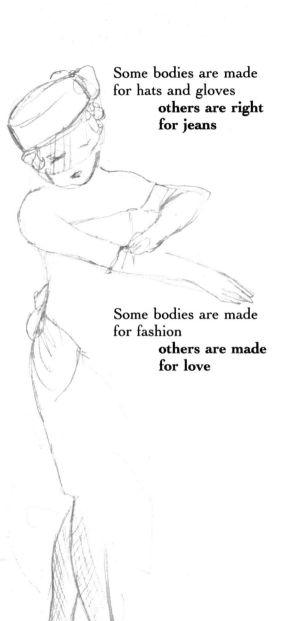

Some bodies are made
for hats and gloves
**others are right
for jeans**

Some bodies are made
for fashion
**others are made
for love**

Wrong Century

If I lived in the time of
Rembrandt or Rubens or Renoir
When women had full breasts,
large buttocks and big thighs
where dimples and folds,
were considered beautiful
If I were living then
I would be much too thin

But I live in the time of
Harper's Bazaar and *Vogue* magazine
and so I'm too fat!

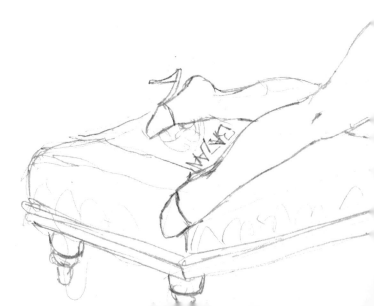

Half the Fun?

"Getting there
is half the fun!"

**Not if you're
on a diet . . .**

Calorie Saver

I'm so glad that cake was tasteless
that the filling was like glue
that the icing looked like toothpaste
I'm so glad

I'm relieved dessert was awful
that the ice cream was too sweet
that the cookies were like cardboard
I'm relieved

I didn't eat.

The Celebration

I finally made it
I lost ten pounds
I look terrific
my clothes fit well
even a little too loosely

I have new cheekbones
a smaller waist
can tuck my shirt in
instead of needing a loose blouse
to hide my big hips

How shall I celebrate?

With a triple scoop of ice cream?
A large slice of New York cheesecake?
A big piece of lemon meringue pie?
A huge portion of chocolate mousse?
A whole box of candy?

Oh, well!
I guess I'll have some low-fat cottage cheese
on a small piece of salt-free melba toast!

Addiction

I am an addict
I have a real addiction
it is not alcohol or drugs
it is not smoking
it is food

I love to eat
and even when I'm not hungry
will eat chocolate chip cookies
or hazelnut ice cream

I can gain three pounds
after one good meal
and starve myself
for three weeks
to lose them again

When I'm upset
I eat for comfort
when I'm happy
I eat for joy
when I'm bored
I eat to fill up the time

When I'm tired
I eat to get energy
even when I'm very busy
I eat just in case
I won't have time to later

I am an addict
and live my life
feeling deprived
when I don't indulge
and feeling guilty when I do

Irresistible

I don't know why I take
the hotel stationery
why I take
the leftover soap
and pack their shower cap
when I have my own
why I keep the shampoos
and herbal bath packets
when I never use them at home.

I guess when something's free
I just can't let it be

I'm not sure this is normal behavior
and I'm embarrassed to admit
that I have
a lot of hotel stationery,
shower caps, soap, shampoo
and herbal bath packets at home.

Natasha's Law

Murphy's Law states that
"anything that can go wrong, will
and always at the worst possible moment"

Parkinson's Law says that
"work will expand to fill
all the available time"

The Peter Principle observes that
"everyone rises eventually
to a level of incompetence"

And now hear my discovery:
"possessions will expand
to fill all the available space"

This process is not reversible
possessions don't shrink
when space is reduced

I speak from experience.

I'm So Upset!

I'm so upset!
I gained two pounds
"There is famine in Africa!"

I'm so upset!
My dinner was a flop
"There is a war in South America!"

I'm so upset!
I missed that movie
"A chemical plant is leaking in Europe!"

I'm so upset!
My plane is delayed
"There is a hijacking in the Middle East!"

I'm so upset!
I have a bad cold
"There is an oil spill off our coast!"

I'm so upset!
The weather is awful
"Acid rain is destroying our forests!"

I'm so upset
that so very little
can upset me
so very much.

Knowing and Knowledge

what children know
is soon forgotten
replaced by learning

what women know
is oft discounted
in a man's world

what black people know
is devalued
in a white society

when knowing
is replaced by knowledge
we cut ourselves off
from the truth.

The Benefit of the Doubt

White people are OK
unless they goof
and prove otherwise

Black people are not OK
until the prove themselves
as really OK

And then perhaps
maybe
sometimes
here and there
now and then
once in a while
some black people
may be OK

Might we consider
offering equally
the benefit of our doubts?

Barriers

My friend is black
and I have
a funny shyness
about putting my arm
around her
as I would with a white woman
a reticence
about touching
her thick hair
as I could with a white woman
a hesitation
about talking about being black
afraid to sound
like I'm prying
wanting to respect
her differentness
wanting to bridge it
wanting her friendship
wanting her trust
not sure of being accepted
of being acceptable.

In This Together

I am my sisters' keeper

we're in this together
not to win
not to compete
not to conquer

but to educate
to nurture
to help

we are each the other's keeper
let us celebrate
the power within us all
to make the difference

to change the world.

Civilization?

She makes many small braids
of her frizzy hair
        She perms her hair
        to make it frizzy

She makes chalk marks
on her forehead
paints geometric patterns
on her cheeks
and tattoos her body
in intricate designs
        She paints her eyelids
        blue or green
        lines her eyes with black
        dusts pink on her cheeks
        and paints her lips
        and fingernails bright red

She pierces a hole through her nostrils
extends her earlobes
or her lower lip
and wears tight necklaces
around her throat
to make it longer
        She pierces holes in her earlobes
        walks on high heels
        to make herself taller
        and wears a tight girdle
        around her hips
        to make them smaller

She blackens her teeth
and wears bracelets
around her arms
    She whitens her teeth
    and wears bracelets
    around her wrists

She adorns herself
with feathers,
shells and bones
    She adorns herself
    with shiny metals
    and colored stones

When she gets married
she becomes
his property
    When she gets married
    she's called by
    his name

Her father is rich
he has many goats
she will get a husband
who will hunt for game
    Her father is rich
    he has papers in a box
    she will get a husband
    who will hunt for deals

CIVILIZATION IS IN THE EYE OF THE BEHOLDER!

College Reunions

At graduation we showed photos
of boyfriends and fiancés
and squealed
over engagement rings

At our fifth reunion
we had babies' pictures
and we giggled
at how cute they were

At our tenth reunion
we spoke of PTA meetings
car pooling
and cub scouts

At our twentieth
we compared colleges
where our kids had been
accepted

At our thirtieth
we discussed travel
and talked about
our husbands' jobs

At our fortieth
grandchildren's photos
were duly
passed around

At our fiftieth
we talked of those
who had already died

**Why didn't we ever
talk about ourselves?**

The Return

I thought I would remember
these friends forever
but five years later
I can't recall their names

I thought I would always
know the way to their house
but five years later
I got lost

I thought our shared experiences
would always matter
but five years later
they no longer seem important

The present hangs a veil
over the past
obscuring the details
leaving only
blurred impressions
of what I thought
would remain so clear.

Falling Through the Cracks

I'm often not quite ready
to let go of the past
and so not quite ready
to commit to the future

I'm often
so attached to the old
that I'm not willing
to tackle the new

Some situations are not quite
bad enough to leave
but yet not quite
good enough to stay

However, if I sit too long
between two chairs
I'm in greater danger
of falling right through the crack.

Friend in Need

Today my husband left me
I'm alone
and I feel frightened

Today I went to work
leaving my babies at home
and I feel guilty

Today my boss yelled at me
but I can't yell back
and I feel angry

Today my mother's ill
I have no time for her
and I am worried

Today I couldn't keep up
with all the demands on my time
and I'm exhausted

Today I needed you
my friend
to hold my hand
and let me cry

Tomorrow
when you need me
I will be there
for you.

The OK Person Badge

I am always working on
my "OK Person Badge"
which must be earned
on a continuous basis
the criteria being:

a spotless home
with gourmet meals
fashionable clothes
a devoted husband
well-behaved children
published writings
a good income
flowers in the house
time for friends
knowledgeable about
politics and art
and the latest brain research

Will I ever earn
that "OK Person Badge"?

Even my mother says
I'm improving
I pay my bills on time
invest carefully
save for a rainy day
take my vitamins
stay on a diet
exercise every day
raise money for
the most worthwhile causes
attend all the right luncheons

Trying to be OK enough to earn
my "OK PERSON BADGE."

A Balanced Life

They say one should live
a balanced life.
Mine is totally lopsided.

They say one should find time for
both work and play.
But I'm happy working all day
and sometimes
evenings and weekends.

Life does not have
to be balanced
on a daily basis
or even on a weekly one.

Life can be balanced
sequentially
working hard now
and playing hard
later.

Live Wire

Sometimes I'm angry and upset
and I don't know why
I just have this short fuse
I blow up for nothing
become nasty, impatient
and give the nicest people
a hard time

I hate myself that way
but the strong feelings are there
just under the surface
ready to come out
and hit the next person
I see

Then I feel terrible
I'm guilty, I apologize
and can't understand
what's gotten into me

Most days I'm really nice
It's just once in a while
for no reason at all
unconnected to any event
I lash out
Next time, when I feel that way
I'll put on a sign that says:
"Don't Come Too Close,

LIVE WIRE!"

Now or Never

I want to live purposefully
aware, cognizant, conscious
of the way I live

I want to have a planned life
thought out, thought through
carefully considered

Instead of living from crisis to crisis
responding only to emergencies
taking care of what's most urgent

I don't want to dress in five minutes
gulp down my food in two
be rushed on the phone
scribble curt notes to friends
and run through the house
always late for the next unscheduled event

I want to take time to notice each day
take pleasure in living each hour
I want to enjoy every minute
before it has ticked away.

Afraid to Miss Something

I'm glad I went
although it was
totally uninteresting

Had I not gone
I'd never have known
that I would have missed
nothing.

The Unreachable Goal

When I meet a friend
I haven't seen in a while
I ask, "How are you?"
and after the perfunctory, "Just fine,"
I ask, "What are you doing these days?"
and get a list of the more recent
                        accomplishments.
Then it's my turn to provide
a rundown of my current achievements.

As each friend evaluates
the success of the other
we don't ask how we feel about it all
what prices we're paying for our careers
what they cost our families
we don't ask about what we are thinking
or reading or worrying about.

And after we leave each other
we are relieved to have been able
to measure up once more
to some vague expectations
to some unwritten standard
which keeps moving higher
as we get nearer the goal.

We are perpetually striving
always almost arriving
but never really there.

The Important People

I used to watch
the important people having lunch
wishing I could eat
with them

I used to wonder
what the important people said
wishing I could talk
with them

I wanted to know
where the important people went
wishing I could go
with them

I tried to guess
what the important people did
wishing I could do it
with them

And now that I have lunch with them
and talk with them and go with them
I've discovered that they look important
only from a distance

The important people
are no different from the people
who sat with me
when I used to watch
the important people
having lunch

Risk Taking

Why is it
that when I make a mistake
it's always entirely my fault
and I blame myself
feeling just awful
for being so stupid

but when I have accomplished
something successfully
I don't take any credit
don't pat myself on the back
Instead I say
"I was just lucky!"

You Never Know and Just in Case

"You never know"
and "just in case"
are the two phrases
I live by

So I notice
what seems insignificant
and remember
unimportant events

I do some things
not for the doing
but for the having done

I collect experiences
and live through events
which are not all
especially pleasant

But I keep doing it still
because just in case,
you never know...
something may come in handy.

Mistakes

I never make
the same mistake twice
The problem is
that I can make
so many
once.

Caution!

Lest

the new woman

become

like the old man

Language

Don't say
"I'm lowering my standards"
but say
"I'm shifting my priorities"

Don't speak
of your "intuition"
mention
your "hypothesis"

Don't ask
for "help"
request
a "problem-solving session"

Don't answer
"I was just lucky"
tell them
"I worked hard for it"

Don't admit
"It's just an old dress"
say
"I'm glad you like it"

Don't ever say
"Oh, it was nothing"
say
"Thank you!"

What's in a Word

I say:
"You must play office politics"

She says:
"I don't like to be manipulative"

I say:
"Don't use the word 'manipulation,'
                          use 'strategy'"

She says:
"Oh, then I can do it."

Packing List for Women Entering Traditionally Male-Dominated Jobs*

Take with you:

- a helmet for the knocks
- a cushion for the falls
- a handkerchief for the tears
- sunglasses for the lights directed at you
- earplugs for the gossip
- good shoes for running twice as fast as the others in order to get to the same place
- an umbrella for unexpected storms
- a sweater for sudden chills
- a cool dress to wear when the heat is turned on
- a hammer to nail down promises
- a hatchet to open closed doors
- a key to open closed minds
- an ax to get you through the thickets
- a gavel to command attention
- stilts to raise you to eye level
- a microphone so that you'll be heard
- binoculars to help you see at a distance
- a flashlight to help you see in the dark
- a fire extinguisher for smoldering ashes
- a mop for floodwaters
- a chastity belt for overtime
- a box to pick up the pieces
- and a friend to rely on in need

On your return trip, you will pack:

- a certificate of merit
- a gold star
- the Medal of Honor
- the Purple Heart
- a badge of courage
- and a halo
- for having survived

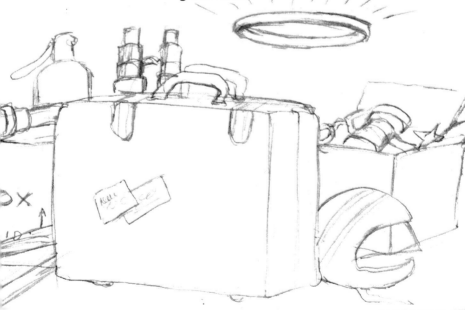

°Adapted from the author's *Paths to Power*.

He Can/She Can't

He smiles at her
he's friendly
     She smiles at him
     she's flirting

He takes her arm
he's protective
     She takes his arm
     she's seductive

He asks her for lunch
he wants to talk business
     She asks him for lunch
     she wants an affair

He pays the bill
he's on an expense account
     She pays the bill
     she's one of those women's libbers

He pats her on the head
he's fatherly
     She pats him on the head
     she's forward

He swears
he's a real man
     She swears
     she's no lady

He tells a dirty joke
he's funny
>   She tells a dirty joke
>   she's crude

He got the big account
he worked hard
>   She got the big account
>   she was lucky

He got a promotion
he's clever
>   She got a promotion
>   she charmed them

His pants are too tight
he gained weight
>   Her skirt is too tight
>   she's asking for it

He's sleeping with her
he scored
>   She's sleeping with him
>   she's a slut

Dress for Success

Nothing too short

Nothing too bright

Nothing too low

Nothing too tight

If One Woman Goofs

If one woman goofs
everyone says
we shouldn't have hired a woman

If ten men goof
no one says
we shouldn't have hired a man!

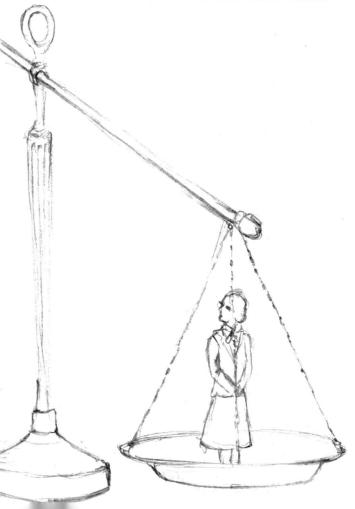

Boys Will Be Boys

A leer
a comment about her legs
a dirty joke
a brush against her
a swear word
with an apology
for the lady present

A conversation that stops
when she comes in
the whispering when she's there
the laughter when she passes by
the relief when she quits

Women just can't take it
they have no sense of humor
and overreact to a little "innocent fun."

To Be "One of Them," You Must

Dislike the cafeteria food
complain about the boss
discount your subordinates
joke about the women
disparage the men
make passes you don't mean

You pay the price of membership
by acting according
to others' expectations
If you conform
you're one of them

And so you become
more like the boys
than the boys themselves

Perhaps that's not
how you want to be
Perhaps you're not
the only one
to feel this way
If you're afraid
to check it out
you're always going to be
just "one of them."

Models

My female model
is my mother
a traditional
non-professional
woman at home
with high standards
on how to run a house

My male models
are the men in the office
working sixty hours a week
because they have
wives like my mother
taking care of everything

If I'm like the men
I have no time for anything
except work
evening meetings
and out-of-town business

If I'm like my mother
I have no time for anything
except keeping the house spotless
having hot meals on time
and chauffeuring the children

The world needs new models.
We must be these models.

No Thanks!

Thank you for the feedback
it always helps to know
what I did wrong

Thanks for the criticism
it's important to tell me
so that I can improve

Thank you for telling me
I made a mistake
so that I can avoid it in the future

Thanks for the negative comment
I need it in order
to do better next time

Thanks, but no thanks
you never tell
what I do right

You never praise me
nor recognize my efforts

You do not notice
when all is well
Thanks, but no thanks!

Communications Upward

If I compliment my boss
he'll think I'm buttering him up
trying to ingratiate myself
The words are: "apple polishing."

If I criticize my boss
he'll wonder who the hell I think I am
telling *him* what to do?
The words are: "the know-it-all."

If I say nothing to my boss
he'll discount me as indifferent,
as a person without opinions
The word is: "invisible."

Apples

If we both have one apple each
I'm happy and all is well
If I have one apple and you have none
I must be better than you
but I may feel a bit guilty
so perhaps I'll give you
a tiny little bite

If you have two apples
and I have but one
it's unfair, not right
undemocratic
I'll join a union
or a movement
start a riot
and kill you for
your extra apple.

Expectations

They told me one hundred people
would come to my lecture
then only forty showed up
and I was disappointed
Had I expected twenty
and twice as many had come
I would have been delighted.

Perceptions

When I was first hired
they said it was through Affirmative Action
When I read my report
they said I had a nice voice
When I voiced my opinion
they said I looked cute
When I discussed the budget
they said I had great legs
When I chaired the committee
they said they liked my dress
When I re-organized the department
they said I had lovely eyes
When I became their manager
they said I slept with the boss.

To the Men at Work

I'm not a chick
or a broad
not even a honey

I'm not a sweetheart
a babe
not either a baby

I'm not a cutie
a darling
not even "your girl"

Don't call me
"hey you"
I have a name too.

Overnight Success

You have to work hard
for years and years
in order to become
a sudden
overnight success

Lose/Win

I have known the pain of
failure
frustration
disappointment
defeat

Because I have taken a chance on
winning
succeeding
achieving

It takes a lot of the first
to get some of the second.

My Typist

I talk into the tape machine
sometimes from an outline
other times from the heart.
From the outline
    the thoughts are better organized
from the heart
    the passion is there.
She picks up the tape
    and in a few days
returns with the typewritten pages
    My manuscript!
I never quite recognize myself
    and seem either
to love it so much I can't change a line
or hate it so I want to throw it out.
But added to the pages
is some special shiny fragment,
    my typist's comments:
what she liked, what she didn't
    and why.
Her own life unfolds through *her* notes
    and we touch each other
silently, secretly.

The Smiling Secretary

Typing
filing
smiling

opening mail
taking dictation
Xeroxing papers
pleasantly

answering the phone
greeting visitors
making reservations
cheerfully

emptying ashtrays
watering plants
with pleasure

with a headache
with a backache
with a sick kid at home

Re-typing
re-filing
re-smiling.

Quiet Desperation

Just like household chores
which are never done
there is always
one more thing
that needs to be cleaned,
cooked, mended
or put away

Work also never gets done
there is always
one more item
that needs to be studied,
written, calculated
or filed away

I'm always catching up
but I'm never "caught up"
when I think I have finished
terminated, accomplished, resolved
there is always still
one more thing
that needs to be done.

The Chance to Reciprocate

If every one of us
who looks good
makes the rest of us
look better
And if the rising tide
lifts all ships

Why do we still compete
instead of helping each other?
Need we keep others down
in order to elevate ourselves?

If I help you today
I will be helped tomorrow
because the world
is not only made up of rivals
but of people who would like
the chance to reciprocate.

A Good Boss Says:

"I can lead you well
only if you tell me how best to lead
you.

I can make the best decisions
only if you keep me informed.

I can prescribe best
if you tell me the consequences.

I need to know
my impact on you.

But I go beyond representing you
beyond being your reflection.

I point out the way to new visions
and to new paths for you to take."

Gut Is Data

Women's guesses
are disparaged
but men's hypotheses
need further research

Women's knowing
carries no weight
but men's knowledge
is significant

Women's feelings
have little value
but men's thoughts
are written down

Women's intuition
is at least as good as
men's hunches.

Right Brain/Left Brain

While the right hand
adds numbers
the left one is doodling

While the right arm
lifts weights
the left is embracing

While the right foot
walks the narrow path
the left one dances a jig

While the right eye
is looking
the left one is seeing

While the right ear
is listening
the left one is hearing

While the left brain
is studying
the right one just "knows."

Hazing

My first day at the job
I'm excited and hope they will like me
Why are they whispering in a corner?

Is it about me?
Did I do something wrong?
They make me nervous.

They're looking at me, laughing
Are my clothes all wrong?
I feel anxious.

They went off to lunch
and left me alone
I cried in the bathroom.

My boss asked how things were going
I said, "Just fine!"
with pounding heart.

My machine broke down
Did someone make it happen?
I'm sick to my stomach.

At the end of the day
no one said good-bye
I don't want to go back.

Familiarity Breeds Promotions

It's not only what you know
but who
it's not only who
but what they are willing to do

Why should they do it?
Because they know you
because you're around
because you're good
publicly, not quietly

When you are close
to the seat of power
it rubs off
like lint
so take a few specks of it
put it on your sleeve
for all to see
that you belong here.

Familiarity
breeds promotions.

Long, Boring Meetings

Long meeting
long and boring
people talking on and on
my eyelids feel heavy
my eyes are closing
in spite of myself

I wiggle my toes
fidget in my chair
draw doodles
chew gum
trying to stay awake

My head is nodding
it falls forward
I startle
have I been asleep?

Maybe no one noticed...

Well-Kept Secret

Woman in charge
strong woman
I know what I'm doing
not afraid to speak out
I get my point across
I look sure of myself
I stand up straight
project my voice
yes, that's me

And yet
and yet
beneath the assertion
a shy little girl
whose voice trembles
whose heart pounds
whose mouth is dry
beneath the assertion
there is a tremulous child
me.

It Isn't Fair!

It is not fair
she wasn't promoted
not because she wasn't good
or smart or effective
but because she wasn't visible
not up-front enough
not taking up enough air time

She was loyal and committed,
worked hard and produced
but that wasn't enough

She was quiet
unobtrusive
working behind the scenes
making things happen
helping others shine
but never took the credit
never asked for recognition

And so
of course she wasn't promoted.

Being Different

At the bottom of the ladder
if you don't dress as they do
don't act as they do
you're a rule breaker
and you will be punished
for being different

At the top of the ladder
if you don't dress as they do
don't act as they do
you're a trendsetter
and you will be rewarded
for being creative.

Quality of Life

I jump out of bed
throw on some clothes
gulp down my coffee
put a note on the fridge
wave to my husband
run out of the house
hop into my car
dash into my office
glance at my mail
scan the paper
scribble a note
get rid of a visitor
cancel a luncheon
order a sandwich
eat at my desk
while I answer the phone
make a rapid decision

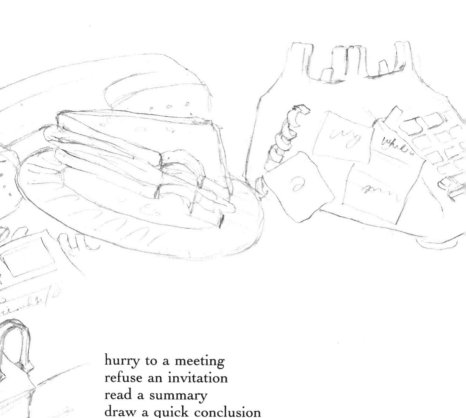

hurry to a meeting
refuse an invitation
read a summary
draw a quick conclusion
speed out of the office
go to a fast-food place
pick up a pizza
throw something in the oven
grab a bite
ask him about his day
not really listen
flip through a journal
skim through a report
turn on the TV
watch a ten-minute newscast
blow him a kiss
hit the sack.

Men's Huts

Brave women are entering
the men's sacred huts
where none have trod before

Some will be eaten by crocodiles
a few will learn the ritual dances
and be accepted by the tribesmen

But outside the village walls
more women wait
to come in.

Am I a "Type A" Personality?

I don't plan my life right

I always wish
I were working less
I wish I were less busy
I dream of one lazy day
with nothing to do

And then, when such a day
without deadlines
or bills to pay
or letters to answer
or drawers to clean
finally happens

I take a walk
read a book
call three friends
eat too much
and wish I had
something to do.

Can't Sleep

Can't sleep
thoughts churning
what I should have said today
but didn't
what I could have done today
but didn't

I toss and turn
not finding
a comfortable position
my head on the pillow
my head under the pillow
on my back
breathing deep
trying to relax

on my stomach
trying to meditate
on my side
trying to visualize peaceful scenes

NOTHING WORKS

I can't sleep
I put my light on
and look at the clock
it's 3:00 a.m.
I must get up at 7:00
that's only four hours' sleep
not enough
I'll be tired all day
I lie awake
worrying that
I can't sleep.

Mediocracy

Mediocrity breeds mediocrity
for in order to survive
it must be afraid of quality

Mediocrity breeds fear
it also breeds bureaucracy
it surrounds itself with rules
afraid of discovery

Mediocrity meets often
and mostly in committees
to create more paperwork
so as to breed more mediocrity.

I Know What I Know

I wish I knew then
what I know now
For I didn't know then
how much I knew
Now I know
what I know
Now I know
that I know.

Someone From Back Home

A familiar face
in an unfamiliar place
even if it's someone
I don't know very well
I rush smiling and hugging
I've found a friend
in a familiar face
I'm not alone
in the unfamiliar place.

Where Is the End of the Line?

Some of us know
where we are going
but most of us
don't know
when we have arrived.

Lists*

On my desk I have several lists:
TO DO:
TO CALL:
TO ORDER:
TO BUY:
TO CHECK:
TO REPAIR:

Why don't I ever make a list of:
good feelings to REMEMBER
special moments to CHERISH
things to be GRATEFUL for
people who have given *me* GIFTS
DAYS OF QUIET.

*Inspired by Wendy Crisp's editorial in *Savvy* magazine.

My Poetry Should

hit your gut
strike your fancy
make you inhale
with recognition
and smile secretly
because *you*
could have written it too